Istio on Pivotal Container Service

Kubernetes cluster with Istio on your own virtual infrastructure

Table of Contents

Preface

Building an Istio enabled Kubernetes cluster on your own infrastructure has some challenges that are not usually well described in official documentations as it often is a combination of multiple environment that causes the issues. This book aims to give some insights as to what is needed to close the gap between official documentation of each software and what we want to achieve in the end.

This is the result on a lot of research and trial-and-error done over the time.

Who should read this book?

Whether you are just curious, or you have extra resources available in your own VMWare infrastructure, if you wish to get started on creating a production ready Kubernetes cluster without paying a cloud provider, this book will help guide you.

Why I wrote this book?

I found myself wanting to experience Kubernetes a bit more and had some resource available, so I tried to set a cluster. I tried multiple ways before finding the one described here like manually creating VMs and installing Kubernetes components, but this is very complicated. I also tried Rancher for a while but was set back by the lack of control in some area. Then I found Pivotal Container Service and liked what it offers, so I started documenting what I was doing and found myself with a little bit more than a blog and here we are.

Convention in this book

Names or labels of link or button will be inserted between quotation marks. Like "Label of button"

Commands to run in a terminal will be marked with a grey background. As such.

There are some Kubernetes YAML files that will have some color and indentation.

Concepts and abbreviations

Here are some of the glossary explained shortly so everyone understands the jargon used in this book. We assume that you have some knowledge of basic networking concepts. There are more concepts in each category that what we list here but these are the ones used in the book.

Generic

HA	High Availability.
FQDN	fully qualified domain name (i.e. www.example.com).
Cluster	A group of machines logically seen as one entity.
NTP	Network Time Protocol
AZ	Availability Zone. Logical location isolation. Usually refer to different physical locations but can be abstracted.

VMWare/vSphere

VM	Virtual Machine.
DRS	Distributed Resource Scheduler.
Resource pool	Logical delimitation of resources. You can limit the number of CPUs or memory on a pool where all VMs within the pool cannot exceed.
OVA/OVF	File that describe a VMWare VM also called templates

Ops/BOSH

UAA	User Account and Authentication.

Kubernetes

Node	Machine (virtual or not) that has a role in Kubernetes.

Master   In Kubernetes, the node(s) that are responsible for the
                  gestion of the cluster. It includes the API, a scheduler and a
                  control manager.
Worker   Here is where your workload will run.
Errand   A VM that is short lived, usually used to perform a specific
                  task then shut down.
Namespace   Logical isolation within Kubernetes. Also used in DNS.
                  N.B: Most of the commonly used objects are defined within
                  a namespace in Kubernetes but some other might cross.
Service   An abstract way to expose a set of pods.
Pod   Smallest deployable unit in Kubernetes. Contains the
                  container(s) you will run. There might be multiple
                  containers in a pod.
Deployment   Description of pods and replicasets that you will run. This is
                  typically a yaml file that you will send to the Kubernetes
                  API to configure your pods/replicas
ReplicaSet   Like deployments but add the possibility to handle the
                  number of identical pods you want to run
DaemonSet   Like replicasets but, instead of defining the number of pods
                  in the yaml file, it will deploy one pod on each worker node
ConfigMap   Files that will hold configuration data
Secret   Like ConfigMaps but data are encrypted
CRD   CustomResourceDefinition. As the name implies, it permits
                  user to create new object definitions as we see fit.
mTLS   Mutual TLS meaning that both side of the connection will
                  have their certificate for authentication.

Introduction

The idea behind this book is that we want to look into creating an environment that would allow us to get our software running as fast and easily as possible when our code is ready. Also, we want some guaranties that there won't be changes from a test environment to the production environment.

Even if we might have more computing power, we do not want to have to change configurations manually. This has to be abstracted. Even if developers are supposed to be DevOps, we do know they usually have minimal experience so we must have something simple for them.

There are also some requirements to high availability, release without downtime and any help we can get from the environment to debug as well as an easy way to see the health of our environment will be positive.

In addition, we do not wish to use a lot of time on maintenance as it would be cheaper to leverage a public cloud in this case.

We are also starting from the fact that our software is based on microservices architecture.

So... how do we get all that?

Challenges

First, let's go through some of the issues that we want to resolve. Overall, we want to simplify the process from a developer completing some code to have it running in production. We assume that we are developping some microservices, even though, if you arc not, the following still applies but to a lesser extend.

Microservices

Starting from the fact that we moved to microservices and cloud native applications, we began to use containers to ship our software. It was a revolution. But we started to see that some larger enterprise applications needed to many of those containers, sometimes we wanted to add multiple instances of a services, we would then need something to balance the load between those services. Service registry, discovery, routing, etc. became a challenge. Here came Kubernetes to orchestrate all this.

It is fine to have all this but there are some things still missing, mainly observability, resilience and security. Some of our services are bound to be expose to the Internet so might get hacked. What happens if someone get access to a pod in our cluster?

Creating a cluster

If you have tried to install a production ready Kubernetes cluster before, you would know of some of the challenges. I find that the main one is that you either have a very complex setup or something that would not be recommended in a production environment. You have multiple tools like Minikube, Docker desktop, Minishift or k3s that are nice and easy if you want to create a simple environment to play with but not applicable to the need of a stable environment.

You could install it manually and there I would say: "good luck" or setting it up with some tool like kubeadmin, but, here, even the installation of the tool itself is hard and you would need good Linux and networking knowledge.

Then you have some wonderful tools like Rancher that will abstract everything and get you up and running in no time but there is a lot of "magic" happening behind the scenes and, as me, you might want to have a little bit more control over what is happening in your cluster.

Also worth noting that, one of my personal requirements is that I want to be able to upgrade my cluster and make some (virtual) hardware changes. What I mean is that I want to be able to add or remove a worker node to the cluster or change the size of the VMs of my worker nodes. All this without downtime.

Getting the LoadBalancer services to get an external IP

As I mentioned, I tried a lot of different solutions to setup a Kubernetes cluster and, in many cases, it was working fine but it was not behind a load balancer that Kubernetes understood so the cluster wouldn't get an IP address. Some tools help you with that others don't. From the official documentation of Kubernetes, it says: "Use a cloud provider like Google Kubernetes Engine or Amazon Web Services to create a Kubernetes cluster. This tutorial creates an external load balancer, which requires a cloud provider."

SSL

With Security being more and more important on the Web, running your site with HTTPS is becoming a requirement. So all web endpoints would need to have their certificates. On a larger cluster, you might have quite a lot of those and that becomes a hassle to update them. Furthermore, you might have heard of Let's Encrypt to get free certificates but they do have a short validity period (3 month) so how do you maintain all these? How can you be sure to never miss one?

Advanced software package install

We all have some well-known software that we want to install but, in this new environment, how do we do it? Imagine that we want to have a master/slave configuration of a database. We know they provide a containerized version of the software but how is the more advanced setup for a production ready cluster?

Goal

As software development moved more and more towards DevOps, we have seen more developers being asked to take care of operations and, from the challenges we just saw, it is not a simple task for any developers. So, our goal is to provide a platform where new software can be launched easily when it is ready with minimal impact or overhead.

If your company already has a private cloud, we want to reuse the existing infrastructure before binding ourselves to another cloud provider. Yes, it would be easier but it might also get expensive over time. A tiny cluster will probably end up around 1500$ a month so if you have some processing power available, this book will give you a way to use it.

What we will do

In this example, we will assume that we are running a vSphere cluster that meets the requirements (see chapter about requirements for details) and will:
- Install Pivotal Ops Manager (v2.8.5) and the BOSH director
- Install PKS (v1.7.0)
- Create new Kubernetes clusters with 3 worker nodes
- Setup the tools to interact with the cluster
- Install a bare metal load balancer
- Install Istio
- Setup cert-manager to get SSL certificate
- Give some examples on how to setup services
- We will also go through some debugging help
- We will show how you can set up automatic deployment of new software from a build pipeline

Note on VMWare vSphere

VMWare just launched Tanzu and version 7 of ESXi and vSphere. These will integrate better with Kubernetes. You can find some official blogs at https://blogs.vmware.com/vsphere/tag/vsphere-7 to get an idea of the new features. It will probably integrtes better but the upgrade of vSphere both on time and license cost is not an option here so we will not discuss this further in this book.

Why did we choose to go this route?

Why Kubernetes?

As most modern software developers can attest, containers have provided us with dramatically more flexibility for running cloud-native applications on physical and virtual infrastructure. Containers package up the services comprising an application and make them portable across different compute environments, for both dev/test and production use. With containers, it's easy to quickly ramp application instances to match spikes in demand. And because containers draw on resources of the host OS, they are much lighter weight than virtual machines. This means containers make highly efficient use of the underlying server infrastructure.

So far so good. But though the container runtime APIs are well suited to managing individual containers, they're woefully inadequate when it comes to managing applications that might comprise hundreds of containers spread across multiple hosts. Containers need to be managed and connected to the outside world for tasks such as scheduling, load balancing, and distribution, and this is where a container orchestration tool like Kubernetes comes into its own.

Kubernetes provides you with:
- Service discovery and load balancing. It can expose a container using the DNS name or using their own IP address. If traffic to a container is high, Kubernetes is able to load balance and distribute the network traffic so that the deployment is stable.
- Storage orchestration: It allows you to automatically mount a storage system of your choice, such as local storages, public cloud providers, and more.
- Automated rollouts and rollbacks: You can describe the desired state for your deployed containers using Kubernetes, and it can change the actual state to the desired state at a controlled rate. For example, you can automate Kubernetes to create new containers for your

deployment, remove existing containers and adopt all their resources to the new container.
- Automatic bin packing: You provide Kubernetes with a cluster of nodes that it can use to run containerized tasks. You tell Kubernetes how much CPU and memory (RAM) each container needs. Kubernetes can fit containers onto your nodes to make the best use of your resources.
- Self-healing: It restarts containers that fail, replaces containers, kills containers that don't respond to your user-defined health check, and doesn't advertise them to clients until they are ready to serve.
- Secret and configuration management: It lets you store and manage sensitive information, such as passwords, OAuth tokens, and SSH keys. You can deploy and update secrets and application configuration without rebuilding your container images, and without exposing secrets in your stack configuration.

You might ask if there are other, better options available. And I would answer that there are others but I could not find better. You might have heard of Rancher, Nomad or Docker Swarm, even Apache Mesos but, in my humble opinion, Kubernetes is still better. Comparing to Nomad and Swarm, it offers much more features. I think that Mesos is more complicated to set up. Rancher is coming close (as it is built on top of Kubernetes) but I feel that we loose some of the control we have with Kubernetes. It helps you getting started quickly but, in some cases you might want to do something that Rancher cannot handle out of the box and come into unforseen issues.

Why PKS?

Here it is a simple case of integration with the existing environment as well as easiness of set up. As we started from available resources on a vSphere environment, we wanted our installation to support as much as possible of the underlying framework.

PKS, now that Pivotal is part of VMWare, is very well integrated and documented. The configuration "wizards" are intuitive if you have minimal knowledge of VMWare vSphere. Comparing to others, you can feel that vSphere is the essential part they want to cover rather than the 5th one they created to add some functionality to a product.

And, obviously much easier than creating all VMs manually.

It also has nice functionality to create multiple plans, good security handling and in-place update/upgrade of cluster without downtime.

Why Istio?

Even though Kubernetes handles many of the issues created by microservices, it does not resolve all of them. For each service, there are some much needed functionality that you would usually want like logging, monitoring or traceability between services. Also, you might want to encrypt traffic between services. Here comes the concept of service mesh. Most of the Kubernetes service mesh will propose a solution for connectivity, security and monitoring.

I would say that there are 3 competitors when looking at service mesh for Kubernetes. Istio, Linkerd and Consul. Comparing the functionality of the 3, you could see that they are very close to each other. They all handle mTLS and certificate management; support TCP, HTTP/1.x, HTTP/2 and gRPC; monitoring with Prometheus. However, there are some differences.

- Linkerd do not offer Circuit Breaking nor Rate Limiting and is a bit more limited on distributed tracing. However, it is easier to setup.
- Consul is also a little bit easier to set up if you can accept it as a single point of failure. If not, it is a bit more painful.
- Istio has all the functionality of the others and the possibility to run chaos monkey style of testing which is limited in Linkerd and non-existing in Consul. On the other hand, it is a bit more complex to set up.

Knowing this, I believe that Istio is the most suited tool here and the complexity is not so high that I see it as a drawback.

Requirements

The software we will install requires vSphere version 6.5U2, 6.5U3, 6.7U2 or 6.7U3 to run. We will also need free capacity to run the different VMs that are needed. Here is a table of the requirements for each main component:

VM	CPU	RAM	Storage
PKS	2	8 GB	20 GB
Pivotal Ops Manager	1	8 GB	160 GB
BOSH Director	2	8 GB	16 GB

Each Kubernetes cluster provisioned through Enterprise PKS deploys the VMs listed in the plan you will define later. If you deploy more than one Kubernetes cluster, you must scale your allocated resources appropriately. Enterprise PKS will deploy at least one of each of the VMs listed in this table here with their minimal requirements:

VM	Number	CPU	RAM	Ephemeral Disk	Persistent Disk
Master	1 or 3	2	4 GB	8 GB	5 GB
Worker	1 or more	2	4 GB	8 GB	50 GB
Errand	1	1	1 GB	8 GB	none

Again, these are minimum requirements however the configuration we will use for those VMs will be defined in a plan at a later stage so you might want to think about what your cluster(s) might look like. You may define 13 different plans with pre-defined VMs starting at 1 CPU, 512 MB RAM and 8 GB disk up to 16 CPU, 64 GB RAM and 256 GB of disk. The VM types are predefined and you can choose them from a drop-down in the same style as you might get at AWS or GCP. Here is a screenshot of the possibilities you will get:

nano (cpu: 1, ram: 512 MB, disk: 8 GB)
micro (cpu: 1, ram: 1 GB, disk: 8 GB)
micro.ram (cpu: 2, ram: 1 GB, disk: 8 GB)
small (cpu: 1, ram: 2 GB, disk: 8 GB)
small.disk (cpu: 1, ram: 2 GB, disk: 16 GB)
medium (cpu: 2, ram: 4 GB, disk: 8 GB)
medium.mem (cpu: 1, ram: 8 GB, disk: 8 GB)
medium.disk (cpu: 2, ram: 4 GB, disk: 32 GB)
medium.cpu (cpu: 4, ram: 2 GB, disk: 8 GB)
large (cpu: 2, ram: 8 GB, disk: 16 GB)
large.mem (cpu: 1, ram: 16 GB, disk: 16 GB)
large.disk (cpu: 2, ram: 8 GB, disk: 64 GB)
large.cpu (cpu: 4, ram: 4 GB, disk: 16 GB)
xlarge (cpu: 4, ram: 16 GB, disk: 32 GB)
xlarge.mem (cpu: 2, ram: 32 GB, disk: 32 GB)
xlarge.disk (cpu: 4, ram: 16 GB, disk: 128 GB)
xlarge.cpu (cpu: 8, ram: 8 GB, disk: 32 GB)
2xlarge (cpu: 8, ram: 32 GB, disk: 64 GB)
2xlarge.mem (cpu: 4, ram: 64 GB, disk: 64 GB)
2xlarge.disk (cpu: 8, ram: 32 GB, disk: 256 GB)
2xlarge.cpu (cpu: 16, ram: 16 GB, disk: 64 GB)

For this book, we used 1 master VM with 4 CPU, 16 GB RAM and 32 GB disk and 3 worker nodes with 16 CPU, 16 GB RAM and 64 GB disk. But, again, this will depend on the workload on your cluster. As a rule of thumb, it is alright to have larger worker nodes but:
- there is a limit on the number of pods per node in Kubernetes
- if a service needs HA, it will be in multiple pods but might be on the same node
- adding a new node to the cluster will take more time for bigger nodes

On the other end, keep in mind that you would need more or bigger master if you have many worker nodes

Installing the infrastructure on vSphere

Deploying Ops Manager

Operations Manager is a former Pivotal product that provides a graphical interface to manage the deployment and upgrade of components available from the pivotal network (now integrated into VMWare Tanzu). There are almost 150 deployable services. It offers a web-based interface and information on the virtual machines it creates. Here are the steps to install it.

1. Log into vCenter using the vSphere Client (HTML5).
2. Select the vSphere Datacenter where you are deploying Ops Manager.
3. Create a vSphere cluster, A vSphere cluster is a collection of ESXi hosts and associated virtual machines (VMs) with shared resources and a shared management interface. Follow the steps below to create a vSphere cluster:
   a. Right-click the vSphere Datacenter object.
   b. Select **New Cluster**.
   c. Name the Cluster. For example, Cluster1.
   d. Select **Turn ON vSphere DRS** to enable DRS. Set DRS Automation to **Partially Automated** or **Full Automated**.
   e. Select **Turn ON vSphere HA** to enable vSphere HA.
4. Create a resource pool for the management components in your deployment. Resource pools are vSphere objects used to organize resources.
Note: The management resource pool separates non-HA components such as Ops Manager and BOSH Director. For example, if you deploy Ops Manager for use with PKS, the PKS management plane includes Ops Manager, BOSH Director, the PKS control plane.
Follow the steps below to create a vSphere resource pool:
   a. Right-click the vSphere cluster object that you created.
   b. Select **New Resource Pool**.
   c. Name the resource pool. For example, RP-MGMT.

d. Review the default CPU and Memory settings and adjust if necessary. This is not common.

e. Click **OK**.

You should end up with something like this:

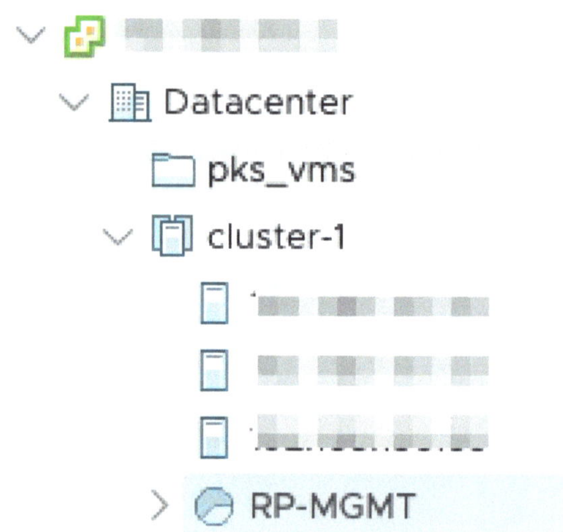

5. Download the Operations Manager OVA file from https://network.pivotal.io/products/ops-manager/

6. Deploy the OVA. Important: set the compute resource to the resource pool created above

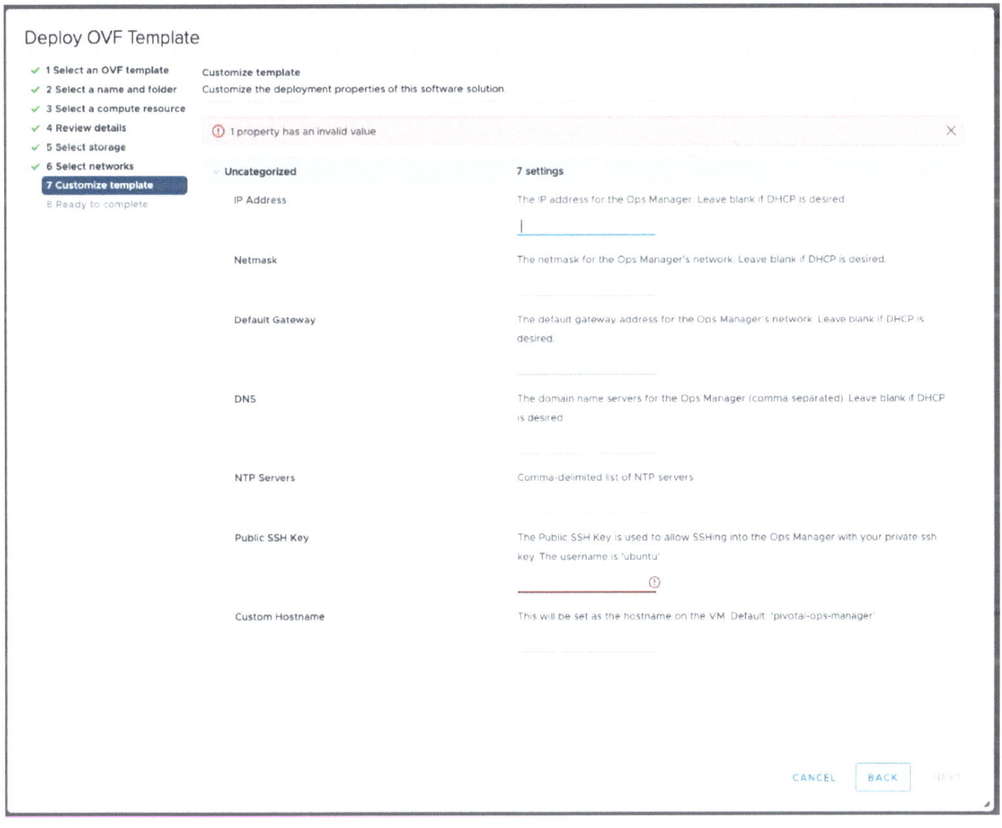

IMPORTANT: Add your SSH public key in the "Customize template" step of the wizard.

Note that the deployment itself will take some time depending on your network but don't be afraid if it takes over 30 minutes. You can monitor the progress in the vSphere client under "Tasks"

7. Add the IP address set in step 6 to your DNS as you must use the fully qualified domain name when you log into Ops Manager.

8. Select the VM created and power it on

9. Navigate to the FQDN of your Ops Manager in a web browser

10. When asked, choose the "Internal Authentication" and create a user

27

Configure the BOSH Director

Before installing PKS, we need to create a bit of infrastructure in the BOSH Director. This is the core component in BOSH. It handles orchastration of the VM creation and deployment, as well as other software and service lifecycle events. The Director creates actionable tasks from different events and add them to a task queue where a worker process will perform those.

To complete the Director configuration, go to your Ops Manager FQDN, login and open the BOSH Director for vSphere tile. It should have an orange bar below the tile. Just click on the tile to navigate to it. You will have, on the left side, the different steps that we need to go through. Optional steps will already be marked with a green tick but I will describe them all here.

vCenter Config

Here you will need to add the configuration for BOSH to connect to vCenter and which resources to use. It is pretty straightforward except the following notes:
- Name: is not important here. It is just the name of the configuration setup
- Datacenter: needs to be the one where you created the cluster and Resource pool earlier
- Datastores: You need to use one that can be accessed from all your nodes in the cluster created earlier
- Folders: The 3 folders you add here need to exist in vCenter

Director Config

Most options here are not needed but you might want to check them out. i.e. backups to S3 is a nice feature but not required. The only required fields are

- NTP servers: add the ones you like. I usually use
  https://www.ntppool.org/en/ to find a pool close to me
- Enable Post Deploy Scripts needs to be checked. Not required by the
  wizard but it is for PKS.

I usually also enable VM Resurrector Plugin and bosh deploy retries as well

Create Availability Zones

You need at least one AZ. Give it a name and add the cluster name and resource pool name we created earlier.

Create Networks

PKS will ask you for a service network as well as an infrastructure network when you will set it up. You will also be asked one for the BOSH Director itself.

Depending on your setup, it might be a good idea to run these on different vSphere adapters and/or different IP range. This is up to you.

The configuration is again straightforward, but you must match exactly the name of the vSphere Network as it is called in vCenter and the IP ranges you defined MUST be available. If the director tries to use an IP in the range, it will check if it is available. If, not the installation of the service you're trying to set up will fail!

Assign AZs and Networks

Here you will choose the AZ and network for the BOSH director. Choose the one that makes sense for your setup.

Security

Here I do not set up a custom certificate but "Include OpsManager Root CA in Trusted Certs" and I generate passwords for each VMs.

BOSH DNS Config

Nothing to note here if you do not have special domain handlers or Recursors

Syslog

Here you can setup a Syslog server for the BOSH Director.

Resource Config

Here you can change the number and size of VMs you want to use. Defaults are fine.

Apply changes

When you make any changes to those configurations, you will need the following steps to apply them:
- Click the "Installation Dashboard" link at the top
- Click "REVIEW PENDING CHANGES" button
- Click "APPLY CHANGES" button and wait for it to complete

Installing Enterprise PKS

PKS enables operators o provision and manage enterprise-grade Kubernetes cluster using BOSH and Ops Manager through the PKS CLI. It offers the possibility of rolling upgrades of the cluster infrastructure, scaling and monitoring and recovery of cluster VMs.

To install it, follow these steps:

1. Download PKS from https://network.pivotal.io/products/pivotal-container-service/ and note where you saved it.
2. Go to the dashboard of your Ops Manager and click "IMPORT A PRODUCT" and choose the file you just downloaded.
3. Now you will see "Enterprise PKS" in the left column, click the plus sign to add it to your staging area.

Configure Enterprisc PKS

There is quite a lot of configuration you will need to setup here and we will go through them now. Remember to click Save after each step before moving to the next. Again, the optional points will already be marked with green ticks as you would not need to change anything but here are some explainations on each step.

Assign AZs and Networks

AZs and Network here are the ones you defined in the BOSH configuration. Simply put, here you'll define in which AZ you want to run singleton jobs and the other jobs so, if you wish, you can have them run in different AZ. Singleton jobs are in only one AZ but the other can run in multiple.

The Network drop downs are a bit confusing in their naming. The one just called "Network" is used for the infrastructure. This is for the PKS API VM. The other one called Service Network is for your actual Kubernetes cluster

PKS API

Here you will give a certificate/key pair for the API. You can click on the "Generate RSA Certificate" below the input area to get Ops Manager to create one for you.

You will also need to set the FQDN of the API hostname.

The "Worker VM Max in Flight" defines how many VMs PKS can start concurrently when creating or resizing a cluster. The default is 4.

Plans

When creating a cluster, PKS will use a plan as a definition of what type of VMs to create and the number of master and worker nodes to set up etc. Keep in mind that the number of worker nodes can be altered when creating a cluster but not much else.

The first one is mandatory and the subsequent ones are optional. This is show with the first radio only allowing you to set the plan as active in Plan 1 whereas the others will let you choose Inactive as well.

There is no solution to what you need to set but the wizard will give you the defaults that are alright for most simple cases. You can also refer to the requirements table earlier to give you some pointers.

One important note here is that the number of masters should be an odd number (1, 3 or 5). Also, obviously, you cannot set a maximum number lower than the number of instances.

At the bottom, you get some optional configuration for draining nodes. Note that if you set **Force node to drain even if pods are still running after timeout**, you will need to set the timeout to a value higher than 0

Kubernetes Cloud Provider

In this book, we are talking about running on vSphere, so this is the one we will choose. You will need to set up your vSphere configuration and remember that the VM Folder need to exist. It will not be created for you. You will also note that PKS supports most public cloud providers as well.

Networking

Here we use Flannel since we do not cover NSX in this book and set CIDR for the Kubernetes pods and services. These network ranges can be different that the ones you use in vSphere and pods and services should also be in different network ranges. Also note that pods will need more IP addresses than services as you might have 1 service for multiple pods.

Usually, you should not need to set up outbound networking nor proxy.

UAA

Here you can set the lifetime of the different tokens for authentication with PKS. Defaults are fine.

Configuring UAA as the OIDC provider or connecting to LDAP or other Identity Provider might make some sense if you have a large organization with this already setup but using the internal UAA without OIDC provider is good enough for us here. However, if you enable OIDC provider, I strongly recommend that you get a valid certificate for the server!

Others

The rest of the configuration is optional and we do not use monitoring, Tanzu Mission Control nor Telemetry. And the default Resource Config is fine.

Performing the installation

Now, that the requirements are in place, go back to the Ops Manager dashboard and click the "Review Pending Changes" button then "APPLY CHANGES".

The initial install will take some time so you can grab a cup of coffee and relax. On my setup it takes usually between 45 and 90 minutes depending on the existing load.

Note on Ops Manager and PKS

There are lot of software available on the pivotal network, have a look at the list to see if there is something that might pique your interest. The ones that integrates with PKS will be marked as such.

I just wanted to note one in particular: The Harbor Registry. It is basically a local docker and helm charts repository that integrates well with PKS. It might be a good fit if you do not have one yet or are paying for one and want to cut some costs. It also have some nice features like repository cleaning and image vulnerability analysis.

Configuring PKS API Load Balancer

Now, in most cases, your environment is behind firewall on a private network however, you might need (or just want) to access PKS from outside. To find out the IP address of the API endpoint, switch to the status tab under Enterprise PKS in your Ops Manager. Now you need to map this IP to an external one in whatever infrastructure you are using. It needs to map TCP 9021 and 8443 ports. The external IP must now be mapped to the FQDN you set earlier.

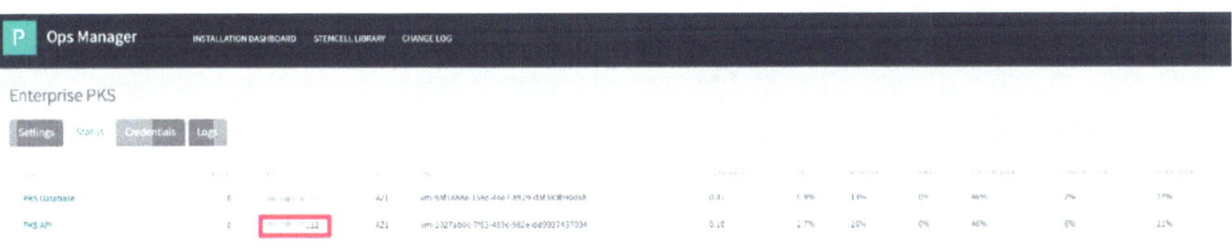

You might have noticed that the title here includes "load balancer" but there does not seem to be a need for it here and you are right. However, we might need it later when setting up the cluster itself if we use multiple master nodes for example. Also knowing that Kubernetes master nodes use the same port (8443), it might be easier to set up a Load Balancer that can map hostname and not only IP. You can always have a different IP for each cluster of course but you might need a lot in the end if you go that way.

If you would like to try one and do not have any yet, I would recommend using HAProxy. It is quite lightweight and performant and do support our requirements here. To give you an idea, here is my configuration for the 8443 port with 3 master nodes.

```
frontend k8s_http
        bind 0.0.0.0:8443 ssl crt /home/user/.acme.sh/example.com/haproxy.pem
        mode http
        redirect scheme https code 301 if !{ ssl_fc }
        option tcplog
```

```
    acl host_k8s_master hdr_beg(host) -i k8s.
    acl host_k8s_pks hdr_beg(host) -i pks.
    use_backend k8s_master_http if host_k8s_master
    use_backend k8s_http if host_k8s_pks


backend k8s_http
    mode http
    option tcplog
    option tcp-check
    balance roundrobin
    default-server inter 10s downinter 5s rise 2 fall 2 slowstart 60s maxconn 250
maxqueue 256 weight 100
    server pks xxx.xxx.xxx.xxx:8443 check ssl verify none


backend k8s_master_http
    mode http
    option tcplog
    option tcp-check
    balance roundrobin
    default-server inter 10s downinter 5s rise 2 fall 2 slowstart 60s maxconn 250
maxqueue 256 weight 100
    server master-0 xxx.xxx.xxx.1:8443 check fall 3 rise 2 ssl verify none
    server master-1 xxx.xxx.xxx.2:8443 check fall 3 rise 2 ssl verify none
    server master-2 xxx.xxx.xxx.3:8443 check fall 3 rise 2 ssl verify none
```

We will show how to get the IPs for the k8s_master_http after we created the cluster.

Create a user in PKS

We will also need to create a user to perform PKS tasks. To do so, first, we will need to get some information so let's go to the PKS tile in the operations manager and click the status tab. Here, note the IP address of the PKS API.

Next click on the credentials tab then the "link to credentials" next to Pks Uaa Management Admin Client and copy the value of secret from the JSON you will see.

Now we can login in with SSH into the Operation Manager with the user "ubuntu" and login as admin in UAA.

```
ssh ubuntu@<ops-manager>
uaac target https://pks.fqdn:8443 --skip-ssl-validation
uaac token client get admin -s <value from secret>
```

Now we can create new users and add permissions so they can use pks CLI

```
uaac user add <username> --emails <email@address> -p <password>
uaac member add pks.clusters.admin <username>
```

The newly created user can now use the pks CLI to administrate any clusters.

Creating the cluster

Now that we have our environment set up, let's create our cluster. First, we need to get the pks command line client from pivotal network. You can download the one you need from https://network.pivotal.io/products/pivotal-container-service/

Depending on your environment, you might need to add the exec bit to the file:

```
chmod +x pks
```

Now we will have to login into PKS server

```
pks login -a pks.example.com -u username -k
```

the k flag means that you allow an unverified certificate. So, if you have created a valid one earlier, you won't need it.
Now, let's create the cluster itself.

```
pks create-cluster demo-cluster --external-hostname k8s.example.com --plan plan1
```

This will create a cluster named "demo-cluster" with the FQDN "k8s.example.com" based on the plan1 that we defined earlier. You can also pass a –num-nodes x to create the cluster with x number of worker nodes.
Note that this might take some time depending on the number of nodes and their size as well as the current load on your vSphere cluster. To check the status, run:

```
pks cluster demo-cluster
```

This will show the last action state as succeeded when it is completed. DO NOT MOVE FORWARD BEFORE IT HAS COMPLETED. You might get weird error because the state of the cluster is not synchronized. You should see something like this:

```
PKS Version:            1.7.0-build.26
Name:                   demo-cluster
K8s Version:            1.16.7
Plan Name:              plan1
UUID:                   d0ae2f90-f6af-4f53-9bf1-714d9fe2056d
Last Action:            CREATE
Last Action State:      succeeded
Last Action Description:  Instance provisioning completed
Kubernetes Master Host:  k8s.example.com
Kubernetes Master Port:  8443
Worker Nodes:            3
Kubernetes Master IP(s): <masters IP addresses>
Network Profile Name:
Kubernetes Profile Name:
Tags:
```

Now that the cluster is created with its nodes, we will fetch the IPs of the master node(s) to add to our load balancer as shown in previous step. You can see those from the previous command as well but the following will show you extra information and I think it is a nice way to introduce some possibilities in our setup.

First we will need to login into the BOSH director. To do so, you will need to fetch the "BOSH Commandline Credentials" from the Credentials tab in the BOSH Director for vSphere in your Ops Manager. It is a JSON string from which you will need the value from the credential key.

Now we can run the commands:

```
ssh ubuntu@<your.ops.manager>
export <value of credentials from json above>
bosh deployments
```

Note the one with name starting with "service-instance_"

```
bosh -d service-instance_xxxxxx vms
```
And note the IP addresses of the VMs called "master". These are the ones we will need to add to our load balancer.

When your load balancer (or another configuration) is in place, run

```
pks get-credentials demo-cluster
```

This will add a configuration to ~/.kube/config so kubectl will be able to connect. Now try a kubectl command to see if it connects properly. i.e. `kubectl get nodes` that will show you your worker nodes.

If you get an error about a wrong certificate, add `insecure-skip-tls-verify: true` the config file in place of `certificate-authority-data: xxxxxxxx`

This is simply because the certificate is auto-generated (self-signed) and does not have a valid CA.

Configuring our cluster

Here we will go through the setup of the different components in the cluster that we would need to have a fully functional Istio with SSL

Setting up the external load balancer

If you have used the services provided by Google or Amazon, it is something that you probably have never thought of but, on a "bare metal" environment, you do not have an internal load balancer out of the box.

Yes. I know we run on a virtual environment but, in this case, "bare metal" is meant as "not in a cloud service".

So, here is one solution I propose for this: MetalLB. As it is mentioned on their web site, it is still quite a young project in the Kubernetes ecosystem however I've run it in multiple clusters without any issues and have no reservation about recommending it.

The installation is pretty straightforward. Just run

```
kubectl apply -f
https://raw.githubusercontent.com/google/metallb/v0.9.3/manifests/namespace.yaml
kubectl apply -f
https://raw.githubusercontent.com/google/metallb/v0.9.3/manifests/metallb.yaml
kubectl create secret generic -n metallb-system memberlist --from-literal=secretkey="$(openssl rand -base64 128)"
```


This will set up the core components of MetalLB. The most important ones are a DaemonSet called "speaker" (doing the actual job) and a Deployment called controller (orchestrating the whole)

Note that the URLs used are the latest current ones but check their website for possible newer versions.

Now, we need to give MetalLB some configuration so that it knows which IPs it can use. We need a ConfigMap for that and here is an example

metallb-config.yaml

```yaml
apiVersion: v1
kind: ConfigMap
metadata:
  namespace: metallb-system
  name: config
data:
  config: |
    address-pools:
    - name: default
      protocol: layer2
      addresses:
      - xxx.xxx.xxx.xxx/28
```

To apply this configuration, run:

```
kubectl apply -f metallb-config.yaml
```

Note that you can set just one IP, a range as start.IP-end-IP or CIDR as shown above. You can also have multiple ranges set up as well. The IPs do not need to be bound to the network interface of your worker nodes either.

Setting up Istio

Now that we have a load balancer that will give our gateway an IP, we can set up Istio.

WARNING: The new Istio 1.5 seems to have issues with the Kubernetes API as it is set up in PKS. Use latest 1.4 for now.

First, we'll download the Istio command line tool istioctl and add it to our PATH. In a terminal window, run:

```
curl -L https://istio.io/downloadIstio | ISTIO_VERSION=1.4.6 sh -
cd istio-1.4.6
export PATH=$PWD/bin:$PATH
```

Now we will use the tool to generate the yaml file we want to import in our cluster. Run:

```
istioctl manifest generate \
--set profile=demo \
--set values.gateways.istio-egressgateway.enabled=false \
--set values.gateways.istio-ingressgateway.sds.enabled=true \
--set values.global.k8sIngress.enabled=true \
--set values.global.k8sIngress.enableHttps=true \
--set values.global.k8sIngress.gatewayName=ingressgateway \
> istio.yaml
```

This will generate a file called istio.yaml with the some configured values we passed in the command. Note that all variables are change using --set on the CLI. Let's get some explanations of the parameters.

1. Profile: there are 4 profiles in Istio that will generate the configuration for different components. Demo will have them all. You can check them out at https://istio.io/docs/setup/additional-setup/config-profiles/. For our case, we need at least the default.

2. We enable SDS for the ingress gateway. SDS stands for Secret Discover Service. This helps for getting SSL auto configured
3. The next 3 enables ingress for HTTPS and gives it a name.
4. We disable the egress gateway
5. And save to a file

Now that we have a file, we can use kubectl to load it but, before doing so, I recommend splitting the file in 2. The first part stopping after the namespace and serviceaccount are created. You should see it around line 5100 in the file. This because, depending on the power and size of your cluster, some configurations might need a second to be properly sent to all nodes and you might encounter problems when applying. For my setup, it fails around half the time I try to add the whole file at once.

```
kubectl apply -f istio-pre.yaml
kubectl apply -f istio.yaml
```

Let the cluster have some time to set everything up then check with

```
kubectl -n istio-system get pod
```

It will show you when all pods are started. You can also run

```
kubectl -n istio-system get service
```

to show you the services created. Note that istio-ingressgateway should get an external IP as well. This is set by MetalLB. Take note of this IP as it will be the one that your applications deployed in the cluster will be answering to.

If it says Pending for a lot of time, your setup from the previous chapter is not correct.

To make Istio Ingress gateway work with cert-manager (through SDS), you will need to update the generated ingress. Just run:

```
kubectl -n istio-system patch gateway istio-autogenerated-k8s-ingress --type=json
-p='[{"op": "replace", "path": "/spec/servers/1/tls", "value": {"credentialName":
"ingress-cert", "mode": "SIMPLE", "privateKey": "sds", "serverCertificate": "sds"}}]'
```

Auto SSL with cert-manager

cert-manager is a Kubernetes native certificate management controller. It will help handle certificate installation and renewals. It handles everything from certificate requests, orders to update of file in Kubernetes secrets so your services will always be up to date. It also supports wildcard certificates, self-signed or connect to a CA.

There are 2 important concepts here. The "issuer" and the "certificate".

An issuer defines a CA within the cluster that are able to generate certificates. There are 2 types: The Issuer is a resource that is limited to a namespace and the ClusterIssuer that can cross boundaries of a namespace

A certificate will define what your x509 certificate will look like and where to save it. You would typically find the DNS names you want to get a certificate for, which issuer to use and the name of the secret to save the result to.

To install it, just run:

```
kubectl apply --validate=false \
   -f https://github.com/jetstack/cert-manager/releases/download/v0.14.1/cert-manager.yaml
```

Now you have cert-manager installed, verify that all pods are running then we will need to setup an Issuer. In our example, we will define a ClusterIssuer. The only difference is that you would need to change the "Kind" to Issuer and add a namespace to add it to.

We will use let's encrypt to sign our certificates and use the http01 verifying method. Note that this method does not allow wildcard certificates. To do so, you would need dns01 method, but it is not supported for all DNS providers. Check https://cert-manager.io/docs/configuration/acme/dns01/ to get the updated list of supported DNS providers

```yaml
apiVersion: cert-manager.io/v1alpha2
kind: ClusterIssuer
metadata:
  name: letsencrypt-prod
spec:
  acme:
    # The ACME server URL
    server: https://acme-v02.api.letsencrypt.org/directory
    # Email address used for ACME registration
    email: user@example.com
    # Name of a secret used to store the ACME account private key
    privateKeySecretRef:
      name: letsencrypt-prod
    # Enable HTTP01 validations
    solvers:
      - selector:
          dnsZones:
            - 'example.com'
        http01:
          ingress:
            class: istio
```

The most important configuration part here is the ingress class. We are now telling cert-manager to use istio to do its work to generate and verify the certificate. This because cert-manager creates new resources when Let's Encrypt verifies that the domain is valid and it has to know how.

Note that we do not need to give it a dnsZone here, but it will be denied by Let's Encrypt if the zone is not connected to the email account defined here so it is always prudent to have it.

Now, you have the setup to create new certificate automatically in your cluster. It is simply done by creating a configuration with the kind "Certificate". Here is an example:

```yaml
apiVersion: cert-manager.io/v1alpha2
kind: Certificate
metadata:
  name: single-demo-cert
  namespace: istio-system
spec:
  commonName: 'demo.example.com'
  secretName: demo-cert
  renewBefore: 120h
  dnsNames:
    - 'demo.example.com'
    - 'demo2.example.com'
  issuerRef:
    name: letsencrypt-prod
    kind: ClusterIssuer
```

A couple of notes on the configuration.

Certificate needs to be in the namespace it is used so, to make it work with Istio, we add it to the istio-system namespace.

You must set only one common name but can have multiple dnsNames. Keep in mind that the common name is the one people will see first so it might be nicer to have multiple certificates instead of one with a lot of DNS names. The certificate will be set up in the Istio gateway under the configuration of a host. Again, you will be able to set multiple host to use the same configuration, but it is fairly simple to create new ones as well. We will show a complete example of setting up a service in the chapter for elastic system.

Disk

Pods are usually supposed to be quite stateless and do not require persistent storage but, in some cases, it is important to keep data through a restart of a pod. i.e. a database pod.

Kubernetes has the concept of Volumes that are basically filesystem that you can mount in a container in a pod. There are multiple kind of Volumes. For example, to get the certificate in the previous chapter, there will be mounted a volume base on the Secret created by cert-manager where the data for the certificate private and public key will be stored. Same goes for ConfigMaps. Those are generally read-only filesystems. But here we want to get a persistent disk that we can read and write to. These are called PersistentVolumes. Those volumes are created based on a StorageClass and are mapped in a deployment (description of the pod) by a PersistentVolumeClaim. Most of the software that require persistent volumes will have those claims defined already and, if not otherwise specified, the claims will use the StorageClass defined as default in the cluster. This is what we now need to do. Here is a standard configuration for a storage class in vSphere

```
kind: StorageClass
apiVersion: storage.k8s.io/v1
metadata:
  name: thin-disk
  annotations:
    storageclass.kubernetes.io/is-default-class: "true"
provisioner: kubernetes.io/vsphere-volume
parameters:
  datastore: DATASTORE-SAN1
  diskformat: thin
  fstype: ext4
```

Note that we have the annotation mentioning this is the default one and we use thin disk formatted as ext4. This means that, when a pod request a persistent volume, it will create a vmdk (VMWare disk) in the datastore configured here that will be mounted in the pod when it starts.

Note that these volumes in ReadWriteOnce mode. This means that only one pod can mount one volume at a time. Also, ext4 file system isn't usable as a shared file system so it would not work on that level either.

Examples of application setup

Here we will show 2 ways to add software from third parties in your cluster. In addition to the usual way of applying yaml files with kubectl, we will show how to use Helm. Helm helps orchestrating advanced configuration by defining Charts that are basically templates for the yaml files that are updated when installing with values from a file. i.e. you can define version of the software, passwords for the software, size of disks, etc. These will depend on the chart itself and will have default values for all the possible variables. There is a public hub to download chart, but many organizations have their own as well.

Setup with Helm

First, you will need the helm CLI. IT can be installed with brew on Mac `brew install helm` but check their website for other possibilities.

Now, we will use a chart from Bitnami. This is a company that provides lots of templates for different well-known software and different platform like AWS and GCP, and is, usually, very reliable.

First, we will download their production value files and make some changes. The file can be downloaded from https://raw.githubusercontent.com/bitnami/charts/master/bitnami/mariadb/values-production.yaml

In the downloaded file, we will change the root password and, under db, add a username, password and change the name of the database. Lower, we will change the size of the persistent volume as well both on master and replica (set the same size on both). You do not

Then we need to add their repository:

```
helm repo add bitnami https://charts.bitnami.com/bitnami
helm install <name> -f values-production.yaml bitnami/mariadb
```

When this last command is run, we will get quite a lot of information in the console that is worth noting. Things like how to connect to the database. URL of the services. This will create a master and a slave MariaDB in the default namespace called <name>-mariadb-master-0 and <name>-mariadb-slave-0.

Setup with kubectl

Here, we will show how to install Elasticsearch, Kibana, APM and Filebeat in a namespace called elastic-system that is Istio enabled. Elastic.co provides a setup for Kubernetes called ECK. So, first, we will create the Istio enabled namespace and add the CRDs for all of their software.

```
kubectl create namespace elastic-system
kubectl label namespace elastic-system istio-injection=enabled
kubectl apply -f https://download.elastic.co/downloads/eck/1.0.1/all-in-one.yaml
```

Now we have a set of new "Kind" we can use when creating objects in Kubernetes. We will go through some of them here. First, let's create our Elasticsearch cluster. Here is the file we will apply:

```
apiVersion: elasticsearch.k8s.elastic.co/v1
kind: Elasticsearch
metadata:
  namespace: elastic-system
  name: elastic-istio
spec:
  version: 7.6.1
  http:
    tls:
      selfSignedCertificate:
        disabled: true
  nodeSets:
   - name: default
     count: 3
```

```yaml
config:
  node.store.allow_mmap: false
podTemplate:
  metadata:
    annotations:
      traffic.sidecar.istio.io/excludeOutboundPorts: "9300"
      traffic.sidecar.istio.io/excludeInboundPorts: "9300"
```

Note that we have set the cluster to 3 nodes, disabled the self-signed certificate and exclude some ports from istio. The last one is because of the way Elasticsearch is talking between the different nodes to elect a master and check the statuses of the other nodes.

If you need to fetch the password for the elastic user (admin user), you can get it with the following command:

```
kubectl -n elastic-system get secret elastic-istio-es-elastic-user -o=jsonpath='{.data.elastic}' | base64 --decode
```

Now, wait for 2-3 minutes so the Elasticsearch pods are starting before continuing then let's set up Kibana. Again, just a simple file to apply with kubectl:

```yaml
apiVersion: kibana.k8s.elastic.co/v1
kind: Kibana
metadata:
  namespace: elastic-system
  name: elastic-istio
spec:
  version: 7.6.1
  count: 1
  elasticsearchRef:
    name: elastic-istio
  http:
```

```
  tls:
    selfSignedCertificate:
      disabled: true
  podTemplate:
    metadata:
      annotations:
        sidecar.istio.io/rewriteAppHTTPProbers: "true"
```

Here we have only one node, still disabled the self-signed certificate and the last line is to automatically re-write the health checks to go through the proxy. Also note how it knows how to connect to Elasticsearch through the elasticsearchRef. This is the name we gave the Elasticsearch cluster in the previous step. You could also add the APM server with the same file by just changing the Kind to "ApmServer".

Exposing a service with SSL example

Now that we have a cluster with some services, Istio setup and cert-manager in place, let's see how we can reach a service with SSL certificate signed by Let's Encrypt. We will use our Kibana server.

What we need to do to achieve this, is to setup an Istio Gateway and VirtualService as well as a cert-manager Certificate.

Exposing a service to the web

Istio Gateway

Here is the file to apply to setup the gateway:

```yaml
apiVersion: networking.istio.io/v1alpha3
kind: Gateway
metadata:
  name: kibana-gateway
  namespace: istio-system
spec:
  selector:
    istio: ingressgateway # use istio default controller
  servers:
    - hosts:
        - "kibana.example.com"
      port:
        number: 80
        name: http-kibana
        protocol: HTTP
    - hosts:
```

```yaml
    - "kibana.example.com"
  port:
    name: https-kibana
    number: 443
    protocol: https
  tls:
    mode: SIMPLE
    credentialName: kibana-cert
```

Important: The Gateway should reside in the same namespace as the Istio services and the credentialName set here must be the same name used when we will create the certificate.

Istio VirtualService

Now that we have our gateway, let's create the VirtualService. Here is the file to apply:

```yaml
apiVersion: networking.istio.io/v1alpha3
kind: VirtualService
metadata:
  name: kibana
  namespace: elastic-system
spec:
  hosts:
  - "kibana.example.com"
  gateways:
  - istio-system/kibana-gateway
  http:
  - match:
    - uri:
        prefix: /
    route:
```

```yaml
    - destination:
        host: elastic-istio-kb-http.elastic-system.svc.cluster.local
        port:
          number: 5601
```

The gateway here needs to be "prefixed" with the namespace since they are in different ones. The port is the one exposed by the Kibana service and the host is in the usual Kubernetes format

<service name>.<namespace>.svc.cluster.local

Now that we have that in place, if your setup is correct (meaning that kibana.example.com points to the IP of the Istio Ingress Gateway), you will be able to access the Kibana dashboard from your browser through http://kibana.example.com

Cert-manager Certificate

Last, but not least, we will add a valid certificate to our setup so we can access https://kibana.example.com through SSL connection. Here is the Certificate file to apply:

```yaml
apiVersion: cert-manager.io/v1alpha2
kind: Certificate
metadata:
  name: single-kibana-cert
  namespace: istio-system
spec:
  commonName: 'kibana.example.com'
  secretName: kibana-cert
  renewBefore: 120h
  dnsNames:
    - 'kibana.example.com'
```

```yaml
  issuerRef:
    name: letsencrypt-prod
    kind: ClusterIssuer
```

Important that the certificate is in the Istio namespace and that the secretName matches the credentialName set in the Gateway. As well as the reference to the issuer should match the issuer created earlier.

We give the certificate its common name and dns names and cert-manager will create a request, an order and go through the verification. It usually takes minute or 2 to get this done. You can check the status with

```
kubectl -n istio-system get certificate
```

When the column "READY" says "TRUE", you will be able to access the Kibana dashboard through https.

Leveraging Kibana for logs with FileBeat

Since we have an Elasticsearch cluster with Kibana installed, we could use it to handle our log files and build searchable index. To do so, we need to send the logs to Elasticsearch from our containers. There are multiple ways to do so and I will show you how to set up FileBeat. FileBeat is also a product from the same company as Elasticsearch so it is well integrated and offers lot of tools.

As usual, we will need to create a service in our cluster. In this precise case, we will use a DaemonSet. If you remember the start of this book, you would know that it guarantees that 1 pod will run on each worker node in our cluster. It is nice as we will use the log files on the nodes themselves as data source. First, let's add the correct access rights:

```
apiVersion: rbac.authorization.k8s.io/v1
kind: ClusterRoleBinding
metadata:
  name: filebeat
subjects:
  - kind: ServiceAccount
    name: filebeat
    namespace: elastic-system
roleRef:
  kind: ClusterRole
  name: filebeat
  apiGroup: rbac.authorization.k8s.io
---
apiVersion: rbac.authorization.k8s.io/v1
kind: ClusterRole
metadata:
  name: filebeat
  labels:
    k8s-app: filebeat
```

```yaml
rules:
  - apiGroups: [""] # "" indicates the core API group
    resources:
      - namespaces
      - pods
    verbs:
      - get
      - watch
      - list
---
apiVersion: v1
kind: ServiceAccount
metadata:
  name: filebeat
  namespace: elastic-system
  labels:
    k8s-app: filebeat
```

This creates a service accounts and add some rights that FileBeat would need to read the logs and run the needed pods. After, we need to setup the configuration of FileBeat itself:

```yaml
apiVersion: v1
kind: ConfigMap
metadata:
  name: filebeat-config
  namespace: elastic-system
  labels:
    k8s-app: filebeat
data:
  filebeat.yml: |-
    filebeat.inputs:
    - type: container
```

```yaml
  paths:
    - /var/log/containers/*.log
  processors:
    - add_kubernetes_metadata:
        host: ${NODE_NAME}
        matchers:
        - logs_path:
            logs_path: "/var/log/containers/"

# To enable hints based autodiscover, remove `filebeat.inputs` configuration and uncomment
this:
#filebeat.autodiscover:
#  providers:
#    - type: kubernetes
#      node: ${NODE_NAME}
#      hints.enabled: true
#      hints.default_config:
#        type: container
#        paths:
#          - /var/log/containers/*${data.kubernetes.container.id}.log

processors:
  - add_cloud_metadata:
  - add_host_metadata:

cloud.id: ${ELASTIC_CLOUD_ID}
cloud.auth: ${ELASTIC_CLOUD_AUTH}

output.elasticsearch:
  hosts: ['${ELASTICSEARCH_HOST:elasticsearch}:${ELASTICSEARCH_PORT:9200}']
  username: ${ELASTICSEARCH_USERNAME}
  password: ${ELASTICSEARCH_PASSWORD}
```

This leverages environment variables sets up to read all container logs and add some extra metadata from Kubernetes and the host. To get a full overview of possible configuration, see the official documentation at https://www.elastic.co/guide/en/beats/filebeat/current/index.html

Now that we have our configuration in place, we can create our DaemonSet. Here is the file:

```
apiVersion: apps/v1
kind: DaemonSet
metadata:
  name: filebeat
  namespace: elastic-system
  labels:
    k8s-app: filebeat
spec:
  selector:
    matchLabels:
      k8s-app: filebeat
  template:
    metadata:
      labels:
        k8s-app: filebeat
    spec:
      serviceAccountName: filebeat
      terminationGracePeriodSeconds: 30
      hostNetwork: true
      dnsPolicy: ClusterFirstWithHostNet
      containers:
        - name: filebeat
          image: docker.elastic.co/beats/filebeat:7.6.1
          args: [
            "-c", "/etc/filebeat.yml",
            "-e",
```

```yaml
    ]
env:
  - name: ELASTICSEARCH_HOST
    value: "elastic-istio-es-http"
  - name: ELASTICSEARCH_PORT
    value: "9200"
  - name: ELASTICSEARCH_USERNAME
    value: elastic
  - name: ELASTICSEARCH_PASSWORD
    valueFrom:
      secretKeyRef:
        name: elastic-istio-es-elastic-user
        key: elastic
  - name: ELASTIC_CLOUD_ID
    value:
  - name: ELASTIC_CLOUD_AUTH
    value:
  - name: NODE_NAME
    valueFrom:
      fieldRef:
        fieldPath: spec.nodeName
securityContext:
  runAsUser: 0
  # If using Red Hat OpenShift uncomment this:
  #privileged: true
resources:
  limits:
    memory: 200Mi
  requests:
    cpu: 100m
    memory: 100Mi
volumeMounts:
  - name: config
```

```yaml
        mountPath: /etc/filebeat.yml
        readOnly: true
        subPath: filebeat.yml
      - name: data
        mountPath: /usr/share/filebeat/data
      - name: varlibdockercontainers
        mountPath: /var/lib/docker/containers
        readOnly: true
      - name: varlog
        mountPath: /var/log
        readOnly: true
    volumes:
    - name: config
      configMap:
        defaultMode: 0600
        name: filebeat-config
    - name: varlibdockercontainers
      hostPath:
        path: /var/lib/docker/containers
    - name: varlog
      hostPath:
        path: /var/log
    # data folder stores a registry of read status for all files, so we don't send everything again
    # on a Filebeat pod restart
    - name: data
      hostPath:
        path: /var/lib/filebeat-data
        type: DirectoryOrCreate
```

If you have downloaded a similar file from the official documentation, there are 2 changes of notes.

First, we add it to the elastic-system namespace so it can fetch the secret for the elastic user. Second, we add an extra volume to mount. This is because of the way PKS sets up its node. The log files are soft linked from this extra volume eon the host so we need it, or you will get a soft link that do not point to any file.

Now we have data sent to Elasticsearch, let's set up an index in Kibana to view and search them:

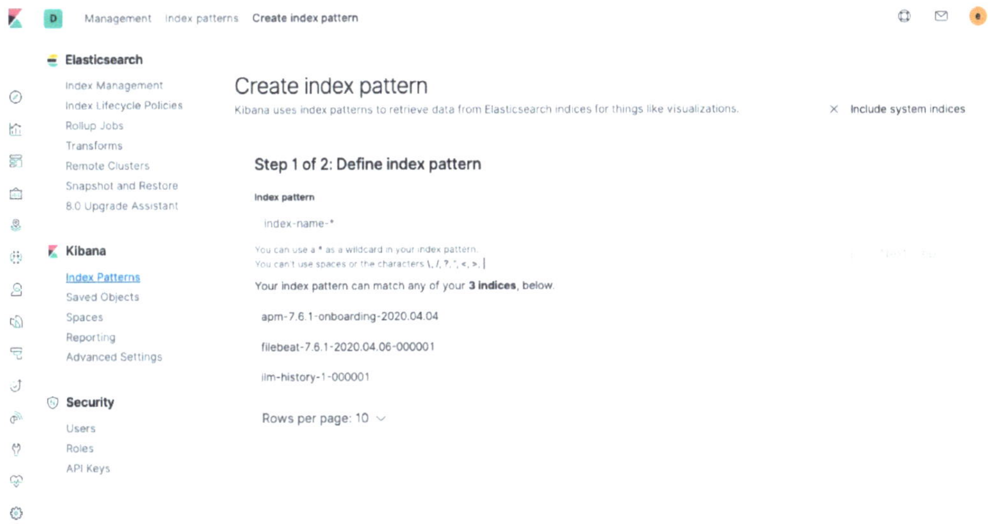

Then add the field that marks the time of the log entry as such:

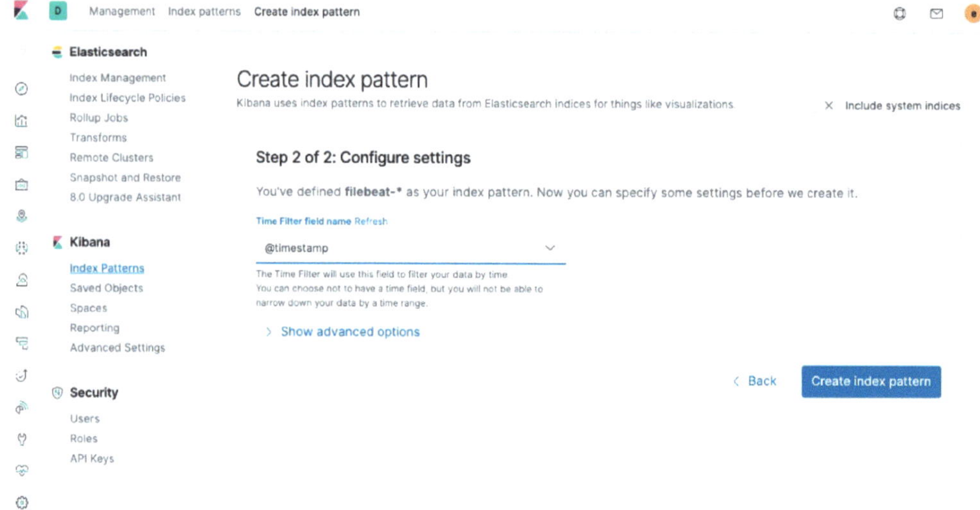

Now we can see and search our log.

You might notice that this includes everything we have in our cluster with a lot of extra metadata so we might want to be more specific in our configuration of FileBeat. Let's say that we wish to create different indices for the different namespaces or skip some. To add an index for each namespace, the end of the config map would look like:

```yaml
output.elasticsearch:
  hosts: ['${ELASTICSEARCH_HOST:elasticsearch}:${ELASTICSEARCH_PORT:9200}']
  username: ${ELASTICSEARCH_USERNAME}
  password: ${ELASTICSEARCH_PASSWORD}
  index: "%{[kubernetes.namespace]:filebeat}-%{+yyyy.MM.dd}"
setup:
  template:
    name: "%{[kubernetes.namespace]:filebeat}"
    pattern: "%{[kubernetes.namespace]:filebeat}-*"
  ilm:
    enabled: false
```

Now you can create a different Kibana view for each namespace.

Add APM monitoring to your applications

A nice tool that you have access to now as part of the Elasticsearch setup is APM that stands for Application Performance Monitoring. It requires a server to aggregate the data and agents loaded in your applications to send data. They have existing agent for Go, Java, .NET, Node.js, Python and Ruby. Being a Java developer, I also really like that it can leverage the standard JVMTI JAVA_TOOL_OPTIONS environment variable so that we do not need to change our Dockerfile to add the agent on startup. First, we will add the server. This is just a simple file to apply with kubectl:

```yaml
apiVersion: apm.k8s.elastic.co/v1
kind: ApmServer
metadata:
  namespace: elastic-system
  name: elastic-istio
spec:
  version: 7.6.1
  count: 1
  elasticsearchRef:
    name: elastic-istio
  http:
    tls:
      selfSignedCertificate:
        disabled: true
  podTemplate:
    metadata:
      annotations:
        sidecar.istio.io/rewriteAppHTTPProbers: "true"
```

This will automatically launch the APM server and configure it to connect with the Kibana instance we already have. Now, in any Deployment you might have and want to add the agent to, we will add an init container that will move the agent to a folder that we will then mount in our application container. Further, we will add some environment variable to the container so it loads the agent and the agent will have the info it needs to know where to send the data.

```yaml
apiVersion: apps/v1
kind: Deployment
metadata:
  name: identity
  namespace: infrastructure
  labels:
    app: identity
spec:
  selector:
    matchLabels:
      app: identity
  replicas: 1
  strategy:
    type: RollingUpdate
    rollingUpdate:
      maxUnavailable: 1
  minReadySeconds: 5
  template:
    metadata:
      labels:
        app: identity
    spec:
      # first create the volumet hat will be shared
      volumes:
        - name: elastic-apm-agent
          emptyDir: {}
      # add the init container that will copy the agent to the volume
      initContainers:
```

```yaml
  - name: elastic-apm-java-agent
    image: docker.elastic.co/observability/apm-agent-java:1.14.0
    volumeMounts:
      - mountPath: /elastic/apm/agent
        name: elastic-apm-agent
    command: ['cp', '-v', '/usr/agent/elastic-apm-agent.jar', '/elastic/apm/agent']
containers:
  - image: example/identity:1.0
    imagePullPolicy: Always
    name: identity
    resources:
      requests:
        memory: "200Mi"
        cpu: "500m"
      limits:
        memory: "1500Mi"
        cpu: "2000m"
    ports:
      - containerPort: 8080
# add the agent to the application container
    volumeMounts:
      - mountPath: /elastic/apm/agent
        name: elastic-apm-agent
# define the env variables to get where the data should be sent to
    env:
      - name: ELASTIC_APM_SERVER_URL
        value: "http://elastic-istio-apm-http.elastic-system.svc.cluster.local:8200"
      - name: ELASTIC_APM_SERVICE_NAME
        value: "identity"
      - name: ELASTIC_APM_APPLICATION_PACKAGES
        value: "com.osnode.auth"
      - name: ELASTIC_APM_ENVIRONMENT
        value: prod
```

```yaml
        - name: ELASTIC_APM_LOG_LEVEL
          value: DEBUG
        - name: ELASTIC_APM_SECRET_TOKEN
          valueFrom:
            secretKeyRef:
              name: elastic-istio-apm-token
              key: secret-token
        # add the JAVA_TOOL_OPTIONS environment variable to be picked up
        - name: JAVA_TOOL_OPTIONS
          value: -javaagent:/elastic/apm/agent/elastic-apm-agent.jar
```

Note that, from this configuration, we are getting a token for the APM server from a secret. This token is in our elastic-system namespace so we need to copy it. Here is a simple way to do so:

```
kubectl -n elastic-system get secret elastic-istio-apm-token --export -o yaml | kubectl apply -n infrastructure -f -
```

Now you can deploy the application and it will send data to the APM server that you can view in Kibana. If you have multiple replicas for this deployment, it will also give you the possibility to see the aggregated data or split it up if you wish.

Tips

DNS setup

You cannot come around the need of some DNS setup when adding a new subdomain for a new application. My recommendation here is to set an A record that will match the external IP address of the istio ingress service then add CNAME records for the new applications.

MetalLB IP pool

With the setup described in this book, you probably would not need more than 1 IP address as all routing is done through Istio but keep in mind that some third-party software you might want to use may need one or might not work well with Istio. On the other hand, those might not be the ones you want to expose to the Web.

Accessing a service or pod not exposed to the Web

In some cases, you might need to access an internal service from your workstation and not expose it through the Web. i.e. our MariaDB in the example earlier. There is a kubectl command that will forward traffic from localhost to your cluster

```
kubectl -n <namespace> port-forward service/<servicename>
<localport>:<portoftheservice>
```

This example is for a service but works also with pods. Just change service to pod/<podname>

Now you can connect to localhost:<localport> and it will access the service or pod you just set.

Deploying updated version of your application

Whatever tool you are using to build your software, you usually want to automate deployment as well. The general idea to do it is to update the image you wish to run in your cluster. If your automatic build tool doesn't support it out of the box, you might just run a kubectl command to do so. Here is how:

```
kubectl -n <namespace> set image deployment <deploymnt name> <container name>=image/image:<new tag>
```

Here is an example of a Jenkinsfile:

```
def shortCommit
pipeline {
  agent any

  stages {
    stage("Checkout") {
      steps {
        script {
          shortCommit = sh(returnStdout: true, script: "git log -n 1 --pretty=format:'%h'").trim()
          echo "${shortCommit}"
        }
      }
    }

    stage("Build") {
      steps {
```

```groovy
            echo 'Building...'
            sh 'do whatever you need to get a new tag with the short commit push’
          }
        }

        stage("Deploy") {
            when {
                branch 'master'
            }
            steps {
                sh "kubectl -n infrastructure set image deployment logger logger=example/logger:${shortCommit}"
            }
        }
    }
}
```

This file will fetch the short version of the commit hash in first step, then we will build it with whatever tool we use. Just make sure that you have the new version pushed to your Docker repository with the short commit hash as its tag.

Lastly, we will update the image in the deployment and Kubernetes will start a new pod with the new version and check that it runs before stopping the old one. Also note that we do this only for the master branch.

You will obviously need to have your Jenkins node with kubectl installed and configured to update your cluster.

Common problems

Error in the Operation Manager

Here, from the top bar, you can see a "change log" link, it is not the release log but the log file of the changes you tried to make to the system. It will provide the logs of each time you pressed the "APPLY CHANGES" button.

Error while installing the BOSH director and or PKS with IP conflict

When installing software, Operation Manager and BOSH ping the IP it wants to assign to a new VM. If it gets a response, the installation will fail. You will need to go back to your network settings and change either the range or set the IP as reserved.

Cannot access a service from the web

First check that your DNS points to the istio ingress gateway for the domain you want to access.

If DNS is correct but you cannot access your domain, check if you can access the service with port forwarding as explained in the previous chapter. If it doesn't work than you have an issue with the service itself, check the log of your container in the pod. If it works, check the log of the istio-proxy container in your pod.

If the istio-proxy log doesn't show anything, then you probably have an issue with your gateway or virtual service configuration.

SSL certificates are not getting issued

There are multiple reasons why that might happen. First check the log of the cert-manager pod to see if there is any information there. The way Let's encrypt works for HTTP verification is that it will look for a file containing a specific text at a specific URL (/.well-known/acme-challenge/<key>. So, if it cannot find it, the issue will be on hold. Cert-manager handles the creation of the file for you, but you might have some configuration error.

First, check that you can access the service from the web (see above) through HTTP. If you can, then it is probably some failure in cert-manager. Check the log of the cert-manager pod to get more information.

Web application available on HTTP but getting connection refused on HTTPS

First, check the 2 steps described above, then verify that the name of the credentials matched the secret names and that the certificates are issued. Also check that you patched the istio ingress with SDS as shown at the end of the istio setup. Also check the log of the ingress-sds container in the ingressgateway pod.

References

Official documentation for PKS: https://docs.pivotal.io/pks
Official documentation for Ops Manager:
https://docs.pivotal.io/platform/ops-manager
BOSH website: https://bosh.io/docs/
HAProxy web site: https://www.haproxy.org/
MetalLB: https://metallb.universe.tf/
Istio: https://istio.io/
Cert-manager: https://cert-manager.io/
Helm: https://helm.sh/
Elastic: https://www.elastic.co/

Acknowledgement

I just want to take a moment to thanks my wife Christel for her patience throughout this work as well as the help and support that she gave me. Thanks you very much.

I also want to thank my good friend Marius for the possibility to use our common infrastructure to test and research the content of this book. I do hope he can also enjoy the benefits.